The Last Dinosaurs

Photography by
Jane Burton

Text by
Dougal Dixon

Artwork of Photographed Reptiles by
Steve Kirk

SCHOLASTIC INC.

New York   Toronto   London   Auckland   Sydney

North American edition first published in 1987 by
Gareth Stevens, Inc.
7221 West Green Tree Road, Milwaukee, WI 53223, USA

US edition copyright © 1987. Based on *The Age of Dinosaurs,* by Jane Burton
and Dougal Dixon, conceived and produced by Eddison/Sadd Editions, London,
and first published in the United Kingdom and Australia by Sphere Books,
London, 1984, and in the United States of America, under the title *Time Exposure,*
by Beaufort Books, New York, 1984.

Copyright © 1987, this format, by Gareth Stevens, Inc.
Artwork illustrations copyright © Eddison/Sadd Editions, 1984.
Photographs copyright © Jane Burton/Bruce Coleman, 1984.
Additional material and illustrations copyright © 1987 by Gareth Stevens, Inc.

Design: Laurie Shock.
Background photography in selected photos: Norman Tomalin, Paul Wakefield,
David Houston.
Photo retouching: Kay Robinson, with the exception of pages 6-7 by Brian Bull.
Line drawings: Laurie Shock and Paul Robinson.
Additional text: MaryLee Knowlton.
Series editors: MaryLee Knowlton & Mark Sachner.
Technical consultant: Diane Gabriel, Assistant Curator of Paleontology,
Milwaukee Public Museum.

Published by Scholastic, Inc., 730 Broadway, New York, NY 10003,
by arrangement with Gareth Stevens, Inc.

ISBN 0-590-41636-7

12 11 10 9 8 7 6 5 4   9/8 0 1 2 3/9
Printed in the U.S.A.   23
First Scholastic Printing, September 1988

CONTENTS

IGUANODON
and
HYPSILOPHODON

Iguanodon is one of the most famous of the dinosaurs. Many *fossil* skeletons, skin *impressions*, and tracks have been found. The tracks show that Iguanodon traveled in herds. Iguanodon was a plant-eater, or *herbivore*. It had a sharp, horn-covered spike for a thumb. The thumb grew as long as 16 inches.

Hypsilophodon was a small, *herbivorous*, *bipedal* dinosaur. Its long, stiff tail may have been used to balance it as it made quick turns. Hypsilophodon had teeth in the sides of its jaw and a sharp, horn-covered beak in front.

IGUANODON (ig-WAH-no-don)

Length: 29 ft (9 m)   Order: Ornithischia

Location: mostly England and northern Europe; also Rumania, Mongolia, North Africa, and North America

HYPSILOPHODON (HIP-sih-LOH-fo-don)

Length: 6 ft (2 m)   Order: Ornithischia

Location: Isle of Wight (England)

These are the skulls of
Iguanodon (1) and
Hypsilophodon (2). The
beak at the front and the
grinding teeth at the back
tell us these dinosaurs
were plant-eaters.

Deinonychus had four toes. One was very small (1). The second carried a huge sickle-shaped claw used in attack (2). The animal walked on just its third and fourth toes.

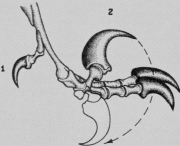

DEINONYCHUS

Deinonychus was discovered in 1964. It was probably a fast, tough, and fierce bipedal *carnivore*. It was lightly built with long-clawed grasping fingers. When it fought, it probably stood on one foot and used its tail for balance. It would then slash out at its *prey* with its sickle-shaped claw.

Remains of five Deinonychus skeletons have been found surrounding the skeleton of another dinosaur. This is evidence that Deinonychus may have hunted in packs.

DEINONYCHUS (di-NONNI-kus)	
Length: 10 ft (3 m)	
Location: Montana	Order: Saurischia

SPINOSAURUS

Spinosaurus was a huge *carnivorous* dinosaur with a fin, or sail, on its back. The sail was formed by strong spines over 6 ft (1.8 m) tall. These spines grew out of the *vertebrae*.

The sail was covered with skin. It was probably used to control the body temperature. The sail may also have helped other animals recognize Spinosaurus either as an enemy or as a member of its own group.

SPINOSAURUS (SPY-no-SAW-rus)

Length: 39 ft (12 m)

Location: Egypt and Niger   Order: Saurischia

Turned at right angles to
the sun, a sail-backed
dinosaur could *absorb*
heat through the fin.
Facing into the sun, the
dinosaur might *radiate*
heat away from its body.

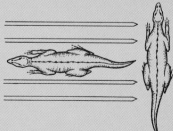

Quetzalcoatlus (1) was a pterosaur. Other kinds of pterosaur are Pteranodon (2), with a wingspan of 23 ft (7 m), and Pterodactylus (3), with a wingspan of 10 inches (25 cm).

QUETZALCOATLUS

Quetzalcoatlus was only discovered in 1971 in Texas. Its wingspan is 39 ft (12 m). This makes it the largest flying animal ever!

Quetzalcoatlus was probably a *scavenger*. Like today's vulture, it would have eaten dead animals. Its body was covered with hair. This hair may have helped it control its temperature. Like vultures, it probably had no hair on its head and neck.

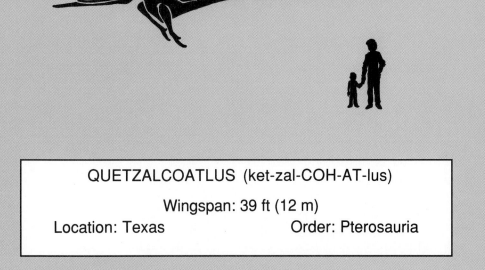

QUETZALCOATLUS (ket-zal-COH-AT-lus)

Wingspan: 39 ft (12 m)

Location: Texas   Order: Pterosauria

STRUTHIOMIMUS

Struthiomimus is known as an "ostrich dinosaur." Its back legs were long and slender and built for speed. It had a long neck, a small skull, large eyes, and a toothless beak. It also had three-fingered hands that were just right for grasping prey.

The "ostrich dinosaurs" traveled in herds. They probably had an *omnivorous* diet of insects, small reptiles, and mammals. They may also have eaten fruit, plants, or the eggs of other dinosaurs.

STRUTHIOMIMUS (stroo-thee-o-MI-mus)	
Length: 13 feet (4 m)	Height: 6 ft (2 m)
Location: Alberta	Order: Saurischia

Struthiomimus outwardly looked like the large flightless birds of today. Scientists feel that Struthiomimus may have run as fast as today's ostrich — perhaps up to 50 mph (80 kph)!

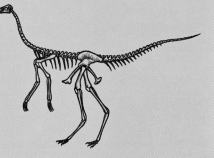

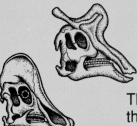

The duck-billed crests of
these dinosaur skulls were
hollow nasal passages that
improved the animals'
sense of smell.

LAMBEOSAURUS

Lambeosaurus was a *crested* duck-billed dinosaur. This herbivore had rows of grinding teeth for eating tough plants, twigs, and pine needles. It could store food in its cheek pouches until the food could be chewed.

Lambeosaurus had strong back legs and smaller front limbs. It had hooves on the three toes of each back leg. Two toes on each front limb had hooves, and two had claws. The front hooves have led scientists to believe that Lambeosaurus often walked on all fours.

LAMBEOSAURUS (lam-bee-o-SAW-rus)

Length: 23 ft (7 m)   Order: Ornithischia
Location: Red Deer River (Alberta, Canada)

PALAEOSCINCUS

Palaeoscincus was one of the first dinosaurs to be discovered in the US. This was in the 1850s. Only the teeth were found. Later, part of a skeleton was found. Palaeoscincus was a squat, tank-like animal with heavy armor on its back. Spikes stuck out from its sides.

With this armor, Palaeoscincus was well-protected from the top. Its underside was unprotected. But not many animals could have turned it over to get at it.

PALAEOSCINCUS (pay-lee-o-SINK-us)

Length: 16 ft (5 m)

Location: Montana   Order: Ornithischia

Like Palaeoscincus, Silvisaurus (1) and Scolosaurus (2) were armored ankylosaurs.

TYRANNOSAURUS

Tyrannosaurus was the largest meat-eating carnivorous dinosaur. Thanks to its huge legs, its five-ton body moved quickly over the ground. Tyrannosaurus may have been more of a scavenger than a *predator*. Its teeth grew up to 6 inches (15 cm) long, and it had a very strong skull. It also had huge neck and jaw muscles. Its strong skull and teeth could have produced enough pressure to crack bones or tear great chunks of flesh.

TYRANNOSAURUS (ty-RAN-o-SAW-rus)

Length: 39 ft (12 m)   Order: Saurischia

Location: Montana and possibly China

Tyrannosaurus could dislocate its jaws like a snake and gulp down great chunks of meat.

PACHYCEPHALOSAURUS

Pachycephalosaurus, or "bone-head," was a bipedal herbivore. It had a keen sense of smell. On top of its head was a thick, bony dome. Pachycephalosaurus probably used its dome for fighting. Like a football helmet, the dome couldn't do much damage, but it could take a lot of battering.

Pachycephalosaurus probably lived in herds. Perhaps head-butting contests took place to see who would lead the herd. These may have been like head-butting contests between mountain sheep of today. When *paleontologists* find Pachycephalosaurus remains, usually only the bony dome is *fossilized*.

PACHYCEPHALOSAURUS
(pack-ee-SEF-ah-lo-SAW-rus)

Length: 16 ft (5 m)   Order: Ornithischia
Location: Montana, Wyoming, and South Dakota

The bony dome of
Pachycephalosaurus was
up to 10 inches (25 cm)
thick and had spikes on
the nose and back of the
skull.

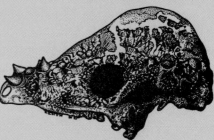

Fifteen different types of Triceratops skull have been found. Here are four of them: 1) brevicornis, 2) elatus, 3) serratus, and 4) albertiensis.

TRICERATOPS

Triceratops is one of the best-known dinosaurs. It was also one of the last. Its head had two eye horns, a nose horn, and a huge *frill* that went over its back. Fossil remains show that it used its head as a weapon.

Triceratops was herbivorous. It nipped off shoots with its hooked beak. Its back teeth worked like scissors. They chopped up food and churned it around inside the cheek pouches.

Triceratops lived on the northern *continents*. As the Earth became cooler, plant life changed. As finding food became harder, Triceratops would become extinct.

TRICERATOPS (try-SARA-tops)	
Length: 36 ft (11 m)	Weight: 8-9 tons
Length of skull: 6 ft (2 m)	Location: Wyoming,
Order: Ornithischia	Colorado, Montana,
	and Saskatchewan

The Red Deer River in Alberta is the site of many dinosaur findings. Styracosaurus, Struthiomimus, and Lambeosaurus are among the dinosaurs discovered there.

Canada

STYRACOSAURUS

Styracosaurus had unusual decorations on its body. It had a very large skull with a long nose horn and short eye horns. The skull could be as long as one-third the length of the body. Styracosaurus had six large spikes on the back edge of its frill. These spikes probably weren't used in combat. But they must have frightened enemies when Styracosaurus lowered its head. Styracosaurus nipped off plants with a turtle-like beak, and it chopped them up with huge slicing cheek teeth.

STYRACOSAURUS (sty-RACK-o-SAW-rus)

Length: 17 ft (5 m)   Order: Ornithischia

Location: Red Deer River (Alberta, Canada)

Fun Facts About Dinosaurs

1. Here are some animals that appeared at the time of the last dinosaurs and still exist today:

   paddlefish — Cretaceous period
   primitive grebes — late Cretaceous period
   opossums — late Cretaceous period

2. By the end of the Cretaceous period, the time of the last dinosaurs, most of the continents were close to the positions in which they are today.

3. As far as scientists know now, none of today's animals evolved from the dinosaurs of the Cretaceous period.

4. A Pachycephalosaurus skull could be as thick as 9 inches (23 cm). By comparison, the human skull is around one-fifth of an inch (0.5 cm) thick. This would make the Pachycephalosaurus skull about 45 times as thick as a human skull!

5. Anatosaurus had a toothless bill like a duck's. Where our molars are it had huge rows, or batteries, of more than 2,000 teeth for grinding.

6. Some species of Triceratops had horns above the brow that stuck out 3 ft (1 m).

7. Tyrannosaurus could have swallowed a person whole, if people had existed during the time of Tyrannosaurus!

8. Deinonychus could hold its victim with its hands, stand on one foot and, using its tail as a counterbalance, slash open its victim's underbelly with the sharp sickle-shaped claw on its second toe.

9. Dinosaurs and other prehistoric reptiles are not the only animals to have become extinct. Here are some others: mastodons, mammoths, giant ground sloths, giant beavers, and saber-toothed cats. Today animal protection groups work to save rare and endangered animals. Some endangered species are tree sloths, mountain gorillas, aye-ayes, orangutans, rhinos, tigers, and bison.

10. The animals that we call dinosaurs are actually two subgroups of the group called Archosauria. These two subgroups are Ornithischia, which means "bird-hipped," and Saurischia, which means "lizard-hipped." Both groups include some dinosaurs that walked on two feet and some that walked on four feet. Both groups also include meat-eaters and plant-eaters. The division of dinosaurs into Ornithischia or Saurischia is based on the types of pelvis or hips they have.

11. Both dinosaurs and pterosaurs, which were flying and gliding reptiles, belonged to the group Archosauria. The crocodile of today is also an archosaur.

12. A cold-blooded flesh-eating dinosaur would eat its body weight in food in 60 days. A warm-blooded animal would eat its body weight in six to ten days.

13. In August, 1966, 2,000 fossil dinosaur tracks were discovered in Rocky Hill, Connecticut. Fifteen hundred of them have been reburied for preservation. You can see the remaining 500, which are sheltered by a geodesic dome. The exact type of dinosaur has not yet been identified. It is probably from the early Jurassic period. It is thought to be related to Dilothosaurus, whose remains have been found in Arizona. The fossil site is now called Dinosaur State Park.

More Books About Dinosaurs

Here are some more books about dinosaurs and other animals of their time. If you see any you would like to read, see if your bookstore or library has them.

About Dinosaurs. Morris (Penguin)
The Age of Dinosaurs! Parker (Gareth Stevens)
All New Dinosaurs and Their Friends from the Great Recent Discoveries. Long & Wells (Bellerphon)
Brontosaurus, the Thunder Lizard. Halstead (Western)
Digging Up Dinosaurs. Aliki (Harper & Row)
Dinosaurs. Jackson (National Geographic Society)
Dinosaurs and Other Archosaurs. Zallinger (Random House)
Dinosaurs and Their Young. Freedman (Holiday House)
Dinosaur Time. Parish (Starstream Products)
The First Dinosaurs. Burton / Dixon (Gareth Stevens)
How Did We Find Out About Dinosaurs? Asimov (Avon)
How to Draw Dinosaurs. LaPlaca (Troll)

New Words

Here are some new words from *The Last Dinosaurs*. They appear for the first time in the text in *italics,* just as they appear here.

absorb ....pull or suck up into something
bipedal (bi-PED-al)................walking or moving on two feet
carnivorous
(car-NIV-er-us)
carnivore
(CAR-niv-or)...........................meat-eating
continents ....the major land masses of the earth. North and South America are continents.

crested ....having a bony ridge or a tuft of hair sticking outward from the head

extinct ....died out

fossil (fossilized) ....the remains or traces of a plant or animal. Fossils are preserved in sedimentary rock formations. Sedimentary rocks are rocks that are laid down in water.

frill ....head shield formed of bones of the skull. Probably used to protect the animal's neck and back from attack from above; to scare enemies; and, on males, to attract females.

herbivore
(HER-biv-or)
herbivorous
her-BIV-er-us)..........................a plant-eating animal

impression(s) ....a mark, imprint, or mold made by pressure

omnivorous
(om-NIV-er-us).........................eating a varied diet of plants, meat, insects, and eggs

paleontologists
pay-lee-on-TOL-o-gists)......scientists who study fossils

predator ....an animal that kills and eats other animals

prey ....an animal that is killed for food by another animal

radiate ....to give off or spread out, as a radiator gives off heat

scavenger ....an animal that eats the leftovers or carcasses of other animals

vertebrae (VER-teh-bray)...the bones of the spinal column; plural of *vertebra*

Index and Pronunciation Guide

Note: The use of a capital letter for an animal's name means that it is a specific *type*, or *genus*, of animal—like a Pterodactylus or Triceratops. The use of a lower case, or small, letter means that it is a member of a larger *group* of animals—like ankylosaurs or pterosaurs.